Seeing Jesus in the

Storm

To Aunt Nada -
Such a Wonderful person you are.
God bless you!

Love,
Melissa Berry

Melissa Berry

ISBN 978-1-64458-546-7 (paperback)
ISBN 978-1-64458-547-4 (digital)

Christian Faith Publishing, Inc.
832 Park Avenue
Meadville, PA 16335
www.christianfaithpublishing.com

Unless otherwise indicated, all scripture is quoted from the English Standard Version: the Classic Reference Edition, English Standard Version (ESV), Copyright 2001 by Crossway Bibles, a publishing ministry of Good News Publishers.

Printed in the United States of America

Dedicated to my parents:

John Berry
Ann Berry

"Life isn't about waiting for the storm to pass... it's about learning to dance in the rain."

—*Vivian Greene*

Contents

Introduction

I do not have a degree in theology nor am I a biblical scholar by any means. This book is not an autobiography. However, it encompasses what I have learned from an accumulation of experiences and what Scriptures say regarding trials and hard times or rather the *storms of life*.

I accepted Jesus as Savior at young age and expected my life to be smooth sailing. I thought that things would go my way and everything would just fall into place. I had a picture in my head of how life would play out, and it certainly did not include hard times. As patiently as I waited for things to fall into place, they never did. At one point, I even thought I was cursed because everything in my life kept unraveling and continued into a downward spiral.

Some people just seem to have an easier time in life than others. I wondered where I was in life and why my life did not measure up to everyone else's. I felt alone. I thought God was not with me and that it was just up to me to make it the best I can through this life. Peace was evasive and contentment fleeting. I felt hopeless until I learned to see Jesus in the midst of the storm.

Chances are you have been burdened by problems that seem insurmountable. You have felt the storm's waves raging all around you. You may have felt as if it is impossible to survive the storm. I have good news for you! Jesus is with you in the storm. He has not left you.

Matthew 14:22–33 tells the story of Jesus walking on water in the midst of a storm toward his disciples in a boat. Peter requested to be called out onto the water, so Jesus granted his request. But he did not calm the storm before calling Peter. At first, Peter walked on water. But his focus quickly shifted from Jesus to the storm, and he began to sink. Responding to Peter's cry for help, Jesus saved him.

Verse 31 says, "Jesus immediately reached out his hand and took hold of him." Jesus could have saved him without touching him. However, Jesus personally took Peter by the hand and lifted him to safety. After Jesus saved Peter, he quickly brought Peter's error to his attention: his doubt (vs. 31). However, despite Peter's mistake, Jesus did not fail to save Peter with a personal touch. Then Jesus calmed the storm (vs. 32).

If the truth is known, many people who appear to have everything together may not have such perfect lives. Some people prefer to hide problems and keep up appearances. No one is immune from storms. Money can be lost, marriages fail, families go separate ways, friends may disappear, and tragedy strikes. The list goes on and on.

This book is not about finding an escape from the storms. It is about weathering the storm well and becoming more durable as a result rather than being defeated. This book is about seeing Jesus in the midst of the storm and walking through it with Him. It is about hope for the future because we do not have to walk through storms alone.

When I started writing this book, I prayed about the title. At first, the title *Finding Jesus in the Storm* came to mind. But God quickly told me change the word finding to seeing. Jesus is always present. He does not play hide-and-seek. Surviving the storm is not a matter of "finding" Him. It is a matter of seeing Him and focusing on Him for safe passage through life's storms.

Chapter I
Me: My Own Storm Maker

"For whatever one sows, that will he also reap. For the one who sows to his own flesh will from the flesh reap corruption, but the one who sows to the Spirit will from the Spirit reap eternal life." (Galatians 6:7–8)

Let me preface this chapter by saying that many of the storms in life are not the fault of the individual. Some just cannot be avoided. I will spend a great deal of time later in the book discussing that. But fortunately, some storms are avoidable.

We become very talented at creating our own storms. As a matter of fact, we are masters at it. Destruction takes little to no effort. Yet the opposite is often true about repairing. We want to live our life our own way and do our own thing. But a moment of pleasure can lead to weeks, months, or even years of problems.

There are all kinds of natural consequences in this world. Just as the law of gravity makes exceptions for no one, neither does anyone escape the law of sowing and reaping as explained in Galatians 6:7–8. If you need an A on that exam, study for the test (and pray for recall). If you want to nurture good relationships with the people whom you care about, be careful about handling strife. If you consume illegal drugs, you risk becoming addicted from which all kinds of trouble will quickly follow. You get the picture.

We cannot live our lives thoughtlessly and carelessly and expect things to magically work out. If I continually run a stop sign, I may get away with it a few times. But eventually, I will reap the consequences of my foolish decision and collide with another car. I can't blame God because I hit that car. But it's easier to blame God (or anyone else) than to take responsibility. A child who disregards his parents' warning to not stick his finger in an electrical outlet and receives a painful jolt as a result cannot legitimately blame his parents for the shock. This world is full of dangers both physically and spiritually. We are wise if we heed the warnings God has given us in His word.

When things go wrong, we want to know why. We questioned God, "Why did you let this happen to me?" I'm not saying there is anything wrong with asking God questions. He wants us to bring concerns and worries to Him. In Matthew 11:28, Jesus said, "Come to me, all who labor and are heavy laden, and I will give you rest." We should express our concerns and questions to Him. The danger comes when we feel anger and bitterness toward God, but instead of asking for His help and guidance, turn away from Him. If we continue to avoid Him and feel bitterness, our hearts are likely to become hardened toward Him, the great I Am who has every answer for every need and every situation in our lives.

God is a Holy God without blemish and without sin. He has every right to give us guidelines and rules to follow. He has every right to tell us how to live. He gave us the Bible as an instruction book which tells us how to sow and reap for good and avoid sowing and reaping destruction. When we ignore His instructions, we set ourselves up for failure and even danger. We reap the consequences of our actions. No matter how much we claim promises or quote scriptures, we will not escape consequences of living in disobedience to God's word.

Just as that stop sign was not put in place for the sake of making people stop, God did not give us guidelines just for the sake of making us obey rules. Safety is the purpose of the stop sign. God's word is for our safety and well-being. "Your word is a lamp to my feet and a light to my path" (Psalm 119:105). If we ignore His word, we are needlessly stumbling through this world in darkness. The book of Proverbs is a wonderful example of the difference between a foolish person and a wise person and gives specific instructions on how to act like a wise person and deal with a foolish person. If I act like a fool, I can expect to reap the consequences of a fool. I can avoid a lot of bad sowing and reaping by acting like a wise person. There are many passages in the Bible, including Jesus's teachings, regarding relationships, finances, and really every situation in life. We are wise if we study God's word and abide by it.

If I buy a computer that needs to be assembled but ignore the instructions, how can I put the computer together correctly? We tend to think that we know how to best run our lives. But who actually knows best? The Creator or the creation? The Potter or the clay? If we knew best, our lives would be perfect. We would never fail, commit sin, or fall into problems. But the truth is that we have a desperate need that demands attention more than food or water. Our Father God, the Creator and Sustainer of the whole universe and everything in it, is the answer to our most dire need: the need to know Him, the need to be directed and led by Him. Even if you are rich and intelligent, you still need Him.

God loves us. He is for us. He wants to save us from as much hardship and pain as possible. He gave us His word so that we may know how to avoid eternal damnation without Him. He also gave us His word as a road map to navigate this earthly life in fleshly vessels. If I decide to go an alternate route, I risk getting lost and running into trouble. How lost I become and how much trouble I run into depends on how far off the main course I've ventured and how long I've been traveling an alternate route.

Perhaps the parable in the Bible that best illustrates creating one's own storm is the story of the prodigal son in Luke 15:11–32 which tells the story of a young man who asked his wealthy father for his half of the inheritance now rather than waiting for his father to die. His father granted his request. The son tried to build his life on his own without the father's guidance and ventured down an alternate, dangerous route rather than remain in his father's territory where he was best protected. He had fun for a while. But the natural consequences of his choices claimed their due. He paid the price. It wasn't punishment; his father never caused any of his problems. He removed himself out from under his father's protection, out of his father's territory. He was at the mercy of the one in whose territory he was residing. At that time in his life, it was not his father. His predicament was a result of his own decisions. In desperation, he returned to his father, and his circumstances changed for the better.

Some instances of straying off God's path may be more subtle than the story of the prodigal son. When we go through long periods of ignoring God and His word, we lose sight of Him and the path He has chosen for us. We can become lost without even realizing it.

Several years ago, I was hiking in the mountains of New Mexico with a group of friends. I grew up in North Carolina where the underbrush in the mountains is thicker due to higher humidity and more rainfall. It's easy to keep sight of the trail because all you have to do is follow the bare ground. But the trail was not as evident in the mountains of New Mexico where it is much drier. There was not much growth except for the trees. From what I remember, all the ground was covered in pine needles; there was no clear path. That near fateful morning, we left just after breakfast. It was a clear, sunny day. The weather, temperature, atmosphere of friendship, and everything else about that morning was perfect. Everyone was in a good mood. We had fun joking and talking. After hiking for a few hours, we stopped and took a break. We then decided to head back. The atmosphere of cheerfulness and joking quickly turned to one of somberness as we realized that we had gotten off the trail and had no clue as to our whereabouts. A ranger's dog had followed us. We tried to get him to lead us back. However, it was no use. He was content to follow. We only had a little food and water. I shared my water with the dog. But the main concern was getting back before dark. This happened in October. We were wearing shorts and t-shirts. After the sun goes down, the temperature drops dramatically due to lack of humidity. Exposure to the nighttime elements would mean being at risk of hypothermia.

The name of the trail was Bear Cave because it supposedly led to a bear's cave. So it did not help matters that the idea that we were in a bear's territory rolled around in my head. We decided to split up and search for the trail. The one to find the trail would yell out to the others. Sure enough, someone finally found the trail and called to the rest of us. We followed the sound of his voice until we all met up and followed the trail back.

How many times have we taken our eyes off Jesus and subtly started following the wrong path and were lost before we realized it? It's easier to lose focus of Jesus and ignore him when everything is going well, when we have an atmosphere of peace and calm. But Jesus never takes His eye off us. He is always watching, always faithful, and always calling out to us, especially when we are venturing down the wrong trail. Just as I heard the voice calling out to lead me to the right path in the mountains, Jesus is calling out to us, leading us to the right path. Isaiah 30:21 declares, "And your ears shall hear a word behind you, saying, 'This is the way; walk in it,' when you turn to the right or when you turn to the left."

I have not written any of this out of criticism or judgment but rather from personal experience. Many years ago when I went through a crisis that resulted in a great loss, I felt as if everything was taken out from under me. I asked God why He allowed that to happen. I didn't expect to receive an answer, but He very plainly told me that I had not been living under his protection. I took a good look at myself and examined the way I had been living. Although I had accepted Jesus as Savior, I did not live according to God's word. Like the prodigal, I had strayed. I rarely read my Bible or prayed. I attended church infrequently. I was living in sin. I had ventured far off the right course and traveled the wrong path for many years. That wrong road was paved with emotional pain, depression, and fear. I felt as if I were living in a dark lonely tunnel and couldn't see any way out. The end result of that crisis was my returning home to my heavenly Father for help. I repented and changed the way I live. I now have a daily relationship with Jesus and live under my heavenly Father's territory which provides protection. I still make mistakes; I'm not perfect. But I am wise enough to quickly repent and make sure that I do not venture out from under God's authority and protection. I am very thankful for the crisis. Without it, I know I never would have changed. Even if not paid immediately, it can be a costly decision to ignore God's word.

The good news is that some storms are avoidable. If you walk with God and follow His precepts, He will steer you away from trouble. If He has a call on your life that places you in jeopardy for the sake of advancing His Kingdom, He will be with you every step of the way. You will not go through anything alone no matter what happens. He will not leave you in suffering. God has good plans for you. He knows what is best. He will lead you to the wisest choices.

I cannot go my own way and expect God to follow me. I need to follow God. He intends good for me and you. One of my favorite verses is Jeremiah 29:11. Quoting from the New International Version (NIV): "For I know the plans I have for you declares the Lord, plans to prosper you and not to harm you, plans to give you hope and a future."

There is nothing wrong with quoting scripture. As a matter of fact, it is quite beneficial since it ingrains God's word in your mind. But I'm not going to receive those good plans by claiming the promise or quoting that scripture. I'm going to discover His good plans described in that verse by being obedient and following the road map He provided for me. If I just listen to Him, He'll lead me to His goodness.

Questions for reflection:

1. Has there ever been a time in your life when you veered off God's path for your life? If so, what was the result?
2. Has there been a time in your life when you reaped a negative consequence due to what you had sown?
3. Has there been a time in your life when you reaped a positive consequence due to sowing the right seed?
4. What are some of the lessons you have learned from past mistakes? Are you better off now from learning the lessons?
5. For bonus points: Don't dwell on past mistakes, just keep the lessons in mind.

Chapter II
Discipline: The Dreaded "D" Word

"For the moment all discipline seems painful rather than pleasant, but later it yields the peaceful fruit of righteousness to those who have been trained by it." (Hebrews 12:11)

When I lived in Amarillo, Texas, years ago, I commuted to work on a long desolate road. In the three and a half years I traveled that route, I only saw a law enforcement vehicle once. It happened to be on a day when I passed a slow car in a no passing zone. I normally did not pass in no passing zones, but this car was going very slow. As soon as I had passed the car, I saw a state trooper's car sitting on the side of the road. I pulled over before he even turned on his lights. I knew I was caught and needed to accept responsibility. The ticket was not just a natural consequence. It was discipline set up by society to keep our roads safe. I have no doubt that God was involved. I believe that He put it in that trooper's mind to sit there even if he did not realize that the idea came from God. I never saw law enforcement on that road before or since. But if I had not received the citation and developed a bad habit of passing when I should not, something far worse may have happened. I would much rather learn a lesson the way I did as opposed to being in an accident.

Sometimes, God is the reason for an uncomfortable situation. Instead of just relying on natural consequences, God will construct circumstances in such a way that grabs our attention and sends a message. God is our Father. He is not passive. He is very much at work in our lives. As a Father, He will sometimes discipline. When I searched for verses on discipline, I found many, many verses. Just to name a few:

> "Know then in your heart that as a man disciplines his son, the Lord your God disciplines you." (Deuteronomy 8:5)
>
> Proverbs 3:11–12 says, "My son, do not despise the Lord's discipline or be weary of His reproof, for the Lord reproves him whom he loves, as a father the son in whom he delights."
>
> Proverbs 12:1 states, "Whoever loves discipline loves knowledge, but he who hates reproof is stupid."
>
> "There is severe discipline for him who forsakes the way; whoever hates reproof will die." (Proverbs 15:10)

Verses about discipline are not limited to the Old Testament. Revelation 3:19 says, "Those whom I love, I reprove and discipline, so be zealous and repent." According to 1 Corinthians 11:32, "But when we are judged by the Lord, we are disciplined so that we may not be condemned along with the world."

When we truly understand discipline, we realize that it is not a bad thing. On the contrary, discipline is for our benefit. According to Vine's Complete Expository Dictionary of Old and New Testament Words, the English transliteration for the New Testament word discipline is the Greek word sōphronismos which means "saving the mind." Sōs means safe while phrēn refers to the mind. Hence, "saving the mind" or "an admonishing or calling to soundness of mind or to self-control" is the Greek definition of the word we know as discipline.[1]

God does not discipline because He is angry. Don't get me wrong; God can get angry. But his motive for discipline is not anger. He wants to train our mind to a new way of thinking. When we submit to His discipline, or new way of thinking, we are more equipped to make better decisions and live more fruitful, productive lives. If there is one thing I want you to remember from this chapter, it is the concept that the definition of discipline is to save. God wants to save us from trouble to come.

Not long ago, I was babysitting a five year old. While eating at the table, he got up to use the bathroom. However, he did not wash his hands when finished but instead went back to the table to eat. I instructed him to wash his hands. He simply looked at me and smiled. Without saying a word, I took the tablet in front of his plate that he was watching and walked away. He immediately jumped up from the table and ran to the bathroom as fast as possible, saying, "I'll wash my hands! I'll wash my hands!" He indeed washed his hands. So I put the tablet back in front of his plate. I was not angry at him. I simply wanted to protect him from harm. With that lesson comes a new mind-set that becomes automatic: "I must wash my hands after using the bathroom and before eating." Once we learn that lesson, we automatically wash our hands without thinking about it. How many times has that lesson saved us from serious illness? Probably much more than we realize.

Since getting that ticket from passing that slow car illegally, my mind has been retrained to be more patient in traffic. I did not receive the ticket because the trooper was angry. I received the ticket because I did something wrong and knew better and could have endangered other lives. God deals with us the same way. His goal is to train our brain to think better and utilize sound judgment. He wants to save us from worse consequences.

I have not received another ticket for passing illegally. But admittedly, I have received a couple of speeding citations since the passing ticket. There again, my brain has been retrained to slow down while driving and be more patient. I have learned to adjust my driving to follow the rules of the road thanks to those tickets. I am much more conscious of my speed.

God's discipline is truly for our good. Look at Revelation 3:19 again; God disciplines those He loves. So His discipline proves His love. According to 1 Corinthians 11:32, God disciplines us so that we will not be condemned with the world which proves that not only does He have our good in mind, but He has our eternity in mind. He also knows our future and what lies ahead as Psalm 94:12–13 says, "Blessed is the man whom You discipline, O Lord, and whom You teach out of Your law, to give him rest from days of trouble, until a pit is dug for the wicked."

Let's take a closer look at 1 Corinthians 11:32, "But when we are judged by the Lord, we are disciplined so that we may not be condemned along with the world." Discipline saves us from God's harsher judgment. If there is one thing I cannot stress enough, it's that discipline is a blessing although it may not feel like it at the time.

Reread Hebrews 12:11 at the beginning of this chapter. Discipline produces righteousness. As human beings, we are short-sighted. We tend to only look at the here and now or the very short future. God sees the big picture. He knows our entire future. He is much more interested in our being prepared to meet Him for eternity and the betterment of His Kingdom on earth than for us to be gratified in the here and now. He always has the big picture in mind, not only for just you or me, but for everyone in the entire world. This life does not even last as long as the blink of an eye compared to all eternity. Once we grasp that concept, we will be very glad that God disciplines now. It helps to prepare us for eternity.

Sometimes, it might feel as if wicked people get away with the most. They seem to be able to do as they please. For a while, they get away with their bad deeds. As God's children, He deals with us first. According to 1 Peter 4:17, "For it is time for judgment to begin at the household of God; and if it begins with us, what will be the outcome for those who do not obey the gospel of God?" The Bible says a great deal about God's judgment of the wicked; Psalm 37 is a primary example. There is a day for judgment or condemnation for those who do evil. Better to be disciplined now rather than condemned later.

In Matthew 25:1–13, Jesus told the story of ten virgins who waited together for the bridegroom to come. Five were wise and brought oil for their lamps while the other five were unprepared due to not having oil. The bridegroom came while the five foolish women had left to find oil. The five wise virgins went in with the bridegroom. The others were left out. The foolish virgins were believers;

they expected to go in with the bridegroom (Jesus). They believed he would come. But He took longer than expected so they were not prepared. In this day and age, with all the distractions around us, it is very easy to get lazy spiritually. I'll take God's discipline any day if it means keeping me prepared and ready for His return. His discipline now is mercy.

In Matthew 13, Jesus told the parable of the sower who scattered seeds. Some of the seeds fell among the thorns which Jesus described as the cares and worries of this world which choked the plants and kept them from growing. That described me. My heart was full of thorns which choked and stunted my spiritual growth. It deafened my ears to hear His voice. I started my relationship with the Lord very enthusiastic. But I took my eyes off the Lord for a long time and made many costly decisions. I did not have a daily relationship with Jesus. I rarely prayed. It seemed as if I experienced one defeat after another. Something inside me spoke very clearly, saying, "You can't make it through this world without Me (Jesus)" which I knew was true. At that point, I was so ready to totally surrender my life to Him. When the pressure was so great that I returned to Him for good, God turned the thorns in my heart to flesh. I could more clearly hear His voice and discern His will. Fear gave way to peace. I found deliverance from a lot of sins and bad habits. But that never would have happened had it not been for the difficulties.

If you have felt God's hand of discipline, take heart; do not be dismayed. You are God's child. He disciplines for our good and out of love. If you heed His discipline and learn what needs to be learned, you will be better off and more righteous as a result.

Jesus is fully committed to you. He is in the midst of the storms that you created for yourself. He is in the midst of the storms resulting from discipline. He has not left you. He is right there in front of you. He is fully prepared and ready to take you through those storms. When Peter started sinking in the waves of the storm because he took his eyes off Jesus (Matthew 14:22–33), Jesus never left; he was still in front of Peter. He had a word of correction for Peter afterward. But nevertheless, He saved Peter.

Questions for reflection:

1. What is the purpose for discipline?
2. Name some safety issues that children need to be protected from. What do you do when you see a child whom you are responsible for in danger from their lack of knowledge or self-control?
3. How has your mind been retrained to think more correctly due to discipline, whether the discipline was from God, parents, or other authority figure?
4. Describe a time you have employed discipline without anger to help another understand an important concept. What was the result of the discipline?

Chapter III
Redemption

> "'For a brief moment I abandoned you, but with deep compassion I will bring you back. In a surge of anger I hid my face from you for a moment, but with everlasting kindness I will have compassion on you,' says the Lord your Redeemer."
> (Isaiah 54:7–8, NIV)

We have all failed and ventured off the correct course. We have all created our own storms and suffered natural consequences and discipline at one time or another. There is forgiveness and redemption. God will restore. Just as the father of the prodigal son restored him, provided for his needs, and showered him with love, God will do the same for those who come to Him. There is hope for the future.

> "'I dwell in the high and holy place, and also with him who is of a contrite and lowly spirit, to revive the spirit of the lowly, and to revive the heart of the contrite. For I will not contend forever, nor will I always be angry; for the spirit would grow faint before me, and the breath of life that I made. Because of the iniquity of his unjust gain I was angry, I struck him; I hid my face and was angry, but he went on backsliding in the way of his own heart. I have seen his ways, but I will heal him; I will lead him and restore comfort to him and his mourners, creating the fruit of the lips.

Peace, peace to the far and to the near,' says the
Lord, 'and I will heal him.'" (Isaiah 57:15b–19)

In the above referenced passage, I want you to take note of three
things. First, God lets go of His anger very quickly. As human beings,
we tend to hold on to anger, and we often project that character trait
onto God. But God is not human; He is divine. God does not stay
angry. As the passage says, we would grow faint (weak). Because God
knows that we are unable to withstand His anger, He is willing to
have mercy and forgive. If God stayed angry, we would absolutely be
crushed beneath the weight of His wrath.

Second, being humble draws God's attention. The passage
begins by saying that God "dwells" with those who have a "lowly"
and "contrite" spirit. Someone who is lowly knows their place. They
know their faults and sins. They do not try to hide or cover deficien-
cies. They are also lowly because they know who they are in rela-
tion to Almighty God. Having a reverent fear or respect for God
will endear Him to remain close and dwell with you. Being lowly
leads to being contrite, which means to be remorseful. If I'm lowly, I
know my place is below God. Because I know I'm below God, I have
remorse for disobedience to His word and change my sinful ways. In
other words, confessing sin and getting right with God will restore
your relationship with Him.

Third, God's redemption puts us in a position to be blessed
by Him. The last part of the passage speaks of peace, comfort, and
healing which is indicative of God's blessings. That does not mean
that everything will go our way all the time. It does not mean that we
will never have health or other problems. But it does mean that we
are in a position to be blessed by God. The verses emphasize comfort
and peace which come from not going through hard times alone.
Jesus is always with us. He is right in front of us just as He was in
front of Peter when Peter stepped onto the water during the storm.
Perhaps the biggest blessing God can give us (other than salvation) is
His comfort during the difficult times. I believe that storms will be
weakened and fewer storms erupt as we turn from sinful ways and
experience God's blessings.

The book of Zephaniah in the Old Testament is a short book, only three chapters. The first two chapters and half of the third chapter proclaim God's judgments on Judah and Jerusalem as well as other nations. But the last part of chapter three speaks of God's restoration for His people. I don't think I've ever heard more lovely words than Zephaniah 3:17 (NIV), "The Lord your God is with you, the Mighty Warrior who saves. He will take great delight in you; in his love he will no longer rebuke you, but will rejoice over you with singing."

Have you ever had a beautiful praise song or scripture that speaks of God's goodness stuck in your head that keeps repeating? Perhaps that is God singing over you. Has someone ever spoken a gentle word of encouragement that lifted your spirit when you were down? Perhaps that was God singing over you. Have you ever had a dire need that was met as an answer to prayer? Perhaps that was God singing over you. His singing over us is a sign that He greatly prefers to pour out His love over us rather than His discipline.

Because of Jesus, we are able to experience redemption and love. He paid the penalty for our sins. Ephesians 1:7 says, "In Him we have redemption through his blood, the forgiveness of our trespasses, according to the riches of his grace." Hebrews 9:11–12 says, "But when Christ appeared as a high priest of the good things that have come, then through the greater and more perfect tent (not made with hands, that is, not of this creation) He entered once for all into the holy places, not by means of the blood of goats and calves but by means of his own blood, thus securing an eternal redemption." Want more proof? Check out Psalm 103:11–12, "For as high as the heavens are above the earth, so great is His steadfast love toward those who fear him; as far as the east is from the west, so far does He remove our transgressions from us." And for those who need extra assurance: "The steadfast love of the Lord never ceases; His mercies never come to an end; they are new every morning; great is Your faithfulness" (Lamentations 3:22–23). Scriptures of God's unfailing love and redemption are abundant throughout the Bible. God makes it very clear that He is ready to forgive and restore.

All we have to do is ask for His forgiveness. As 1 John 1:9 says, "If we confess our sins, he is faithful and just to forgive us our sins and to cleanse us from all unrighteousness." We should stop sinful habits and live obedient lives according to God's word. That does not mean that we will never sin again. But we should strive to live as God has instructed in His word.

John 8:1–11 tells a powerful story of redemption. The scribes and Pharisees brought a woman caught in the act of adultery to Jesus. They wanted to stone her and asked Jesus what he had to say. I love Jesus's answer. He told them that the one without sin could throw the first stone. Verse 9 says that they left, one by one, beginning with the older ones. In verse 11, Jesus told the woman that he did not condemn her. He also instructed her to stop sinning.

Jesus's disciple Peter is a wonderful story of redemption. As discussed in the introduction of this book, Jesus saved Peter from the storm when he was about to sink (Matthew 14:22–33) even though Peter doubted Jesus (vs. 31). In John 16:21–23, Jesus told his disciples that he must be killed and rise again on the third day (vs. 21). But Peter rebuked Jesus for saying such things and told him that would not happen. Jesus sharply rebuked Peter, saying, "Get behind me Satan!" (vs. 23). Finally, Luke 22:54–61 speaks of Peter denying Jesus three times after Jesus had been arrested and was taken away to be crucified. But later in John 21:15–18, Jesus redeemed Peter. Jesus asked Peter three times if he loved him. Every time Peter responded yes. Every time, Jesus responded by instructing Peter to feed His sheep. Jesus honored Peter by giving him a task (to feed His sheep). Despite all of Peter's mistakes and failures, Jesus never disowned him. He never took away Peter's discipleship. He never once told him to go away. Through every one of Peter's mistakes, Jesus never abandoned Peter or cast him out. If you mess up and sin again after confessing your sin, the same grace that was there for you in the beginning will continue to be there for you again and again.

Questions for reflection:

1. Are you burdened by the thought of past sin of which you have asked for God's forgiveness? If so, look up scriptures that deal with God's forgiveness (Romans 8:1 is a starting point.) You can even go back over the scriptures in this chapter.
2. Name a scripture that speaks of God's love that has special meaning to you.
3. Name a praise song or hymn that has a special meaning to you.
4. Name a hymn or praise song or scripture that has gotten stuck in your head.
5. Name a time when someone has encouraged you when you were down.
6. Write down blessings in your life: health, family, friends, food, a place to live, etc.

Chapter IV
Avoiding Storms

"For you are my rock and my fortress; and for
your name's sake you lead me and guide me; you
take me out of the net they have hidden for me,
for you are my refuge." (Psalm 31:3–4)

As discussed in the first two chapters, sometimes we either create our
storm or we are experiencing God's discipline. The positive side to
this truth is that some storms are avoidable. Also mentioned previously, God gave us His word as a road map to navigate this life. God
gave us His word not only to understand Him better but also to keep
us safe. He did not give us rules just for the sake of giving rules but
to spare us from harm. We are not helpless bystanders who fall prey
to whatever comes about in this life. We have control over our lives
to heed God's warnings and steer the course of our life according to
His word. We have the ability to make the sound decisions and save
ourselves some trouble.

The first step in avoiding storms is to live in obedience to God's
word. Deuteronomy 28:1 says, "And if you faithfully obey the voice
of the Lord your God, being careful to do all His commandments
that I command you today, the Lord your God will set you high
above all the nations of the earth." In the first part of Leviticus 26,
God describes the numerous blessing that He would bestow upon
the Israelites if they obeyed Him. The second part of the chapter
describes the discipline that would happen if they chose to disobey.
The same God the Israelites served is the same God that we serve
today. After all, God is the same throughout time (Hebrews 13:8).

2 Chronicles 20 gives an account of King Jehoshaphat, a king of Judah who feared the Lord and knew the seriousness of obeying the Lord's commands. In this chapter, Jehoshaphat learned that several armies were coming to fight against him. He fasted, prayed, and sought the Lord's direction and obeyed God's instructions. The Lord gave him great victory in battle. God blessed him because of his obedience. But later in his life, the same chapter gives an account of a time when he made an alliance with Ahaziah, a king of Israel who was wicked. The two kings built a fleet of trading ships. Johoshaphat did not seek the Lord's counsel before allying himself with King Ahaziah. God was displeased, and the ships were wrecked. Not much detail is given between those two accounts. I don't know how much time had passed. I don't know if something changed about Johoshaphat's relationship with the Lord. But apparently, he lost focus of the Lord and did not find it important to consult him before a major decision. Starting off good does not guarantee that we will always be faithful. Displaying right thinking once does not mean that we will automatically make wise decisions every time. A daily personal relationship with the Lord is needed to keep us on the right track.

Not only will obeying God's word keep you out of trouble, but it also endears God's heart to you. He is pleased with people who listen and obey Him. Having a heart after God will lead to more answered prayers. The first reason: when our hearts are aligned with God, our hearts' cry will more likely be according to His will. Secondly, God is inclined to answer the prayers of His obedient children.

> Psalm 34:12–15 says, "What man is there who desires life and loves many days, that he may see good? Keep your tongue from evil and your lips from speaking deceit. Turn away from evil and do good; seek peace and pursue it. The eyes of the Lord are toward the righteous and his ears toward their cry."

There are at least two other places in the Bible that I know of that God says the same thing. 2 Chronicles 16:9a (NIV) says, "For the eyes of the Lord range throughout the earth to strengthen those whose hearts are fully committed to Him." According to 1 Peter 3:12a: "For the eyes of the Lord are on the righteous, and His ears are open to their prayer."

Obedience cannot be accomplished without intimacy or closeness with God. For many years, I tried to live a righteous life of integrity without reading God's word or praying. But I failed miserably. The only way to live a righteous, obedient life is to spend time in God's word and prayer daily. Nothing is more important than seeking God each day. Begin the day with prayer and reading scripture to get your mind in tune with Jesus who is the source of all wisdom for any situation that awaits you during the day. Psalm 5:3 says, "O Lord, in the morning you hear my voice; in the morning I prepare a sacrifice for you and watch." Ask for His guidance and wisdom for each day. And again in the evening seek God in prayer. Thank Him for His faithfulness. Bring concerns from the day to Him. "Let my prayer be counted as incense before you, and the lifting up of my hands as the evening sacrifice!" (Psalm 141:2)

Don't know what to pray? That's OK. Just praise God. Thank Him. Even when we have specific requests, we should start and end prayer by praising Him. Hebrews 13:15 says, "Through Him then let us continually offer up a sacrifice of praise to God, that is, the fruit of lips that acknowledge His name." The scriptures go on and on about the importance of praising God. So praise and worship cannot be overemphasized. Often, after spending ample time in praise, situations, or people come to my mind that I know need attention in prayer. Even when I know what to pray about, sometimes I don't know exactly how to pray. But after spending time in praise and worship, the words just come, and I know how to pray about situations and people.

The book of Esther tells the story of a Jewish girl becoming queen by winning a beauty pageant, so to speak, while the Jews were living in exile. But she was not equal to the king; she was his subordinate. In Esther 5, Esther needs to ask the king for a favor which is all part of a plan to save the Jewish people from eradication. Before she approached the king, she put on her "royal robes" (verse 1). Dressed appropriately to get the king's attention, she stood in the inner court where the king could see from his quarters. When the king saw her, she won his favor. He held out his scepter to her. He asked her what she wanted and even promised to give it to her up to half his kingdom before he even knew her request. Esther put herself in a more favorable position to receive her desired answer from the king by dressing appropriately and by coming to the king respectfully.

I am not advocating that we need to be dressed in our best attire before we pray. Isaiah 61:3 talks about the "garment of praise." Our literal clothes do not matter to God. But we can come to Him with the garment of praise and talk to him respectfully out of reverent submission to Him. We are His children, not His equal. We are subordinate to Him. Are we not more likely to receive a favorable answer when we come to Him dressed in the garment of praise and give Him the respect which He is due?

Wisdom keeps us out of trouble. God is the source of all wisdom which is another reason to pray and read His word daily. James 1:5 assures us that God will provide us with wisdom when we ask.

I formerly struggled with spending money on too many unnecessary things. I would buy something and then feel worried, even to the point of extreme fear, about spending too much money. But I only worried about it weeks later when I was at home and had taken off the tags. This happened several times. I asked God to make me afraid before I buy. After all, that seemed to be the more appropriate time to feel fear. But I never felt fear before making a purchase and would continue to buy. So I asked God why He did not answer that prayer and make me afraid before I buy. He told me (put a "knowing" in my spirit) that He does not lead by fear. He leads by wisdom. I already knew the right thing to do. It was up to me to make the right choice "for God gave us a spirit not of fear but of power and love and *self–control*." 2 Timothy 1:7 (emphasis added).

A major part of wisdom is having the mind of Christ as spoken of in 1 Corinthians 2:16. If we have the mind of Christ, we will think and therefore act more like Christ and avoid foolish decisions. Having the mind of Christ involves asking for wisdom. But to truly have the mind of Christ goes one step farther than asking for wisdom. It means protecting our mind and spirit from what we allow in through the portals of our eyes and ears. Just as foods and drinks that we ingest affect our physical bodies, what we allow in our minds through TV, movies, books, magazines, talk, etc., affect our mind which affects our spiritual well-being. Some food is beneficial for the body and aids in its health and well-being. Some is junk food that is not harmful but should be eaten in moderation. Too much of it can cause a feeling of sluggishness and prevents the body from functioning at optimal level. Some food and drink is poisonous causing serious damage and even death. The same thing is true of the mind/spirit. Music, talk, reading, listening to sermons, etc., that glorifies God promote a Christ-like mind. It's food for the spirit that allows the mind to operate at its best in tune with Jesus. Then there are secular movies, books, magazines, etc., that do not promote a Christ like mind but do hinder it as long as we still spend ample time with God. But too much of it and neglecting time with God can cause a spiritual sluggishness and deafen our ears to His voice. Then there are movies, books, places, and even people that will temp us down a dark path of destruction. They are poison for the mind and spirit and should be avoided at all cost.

2 Kings 22:2 describes King Josiah as one who did right before the Lord and "did not turn aside to the right or to the left." In 2 Kings 23, King Josiah cleansed the temple of the Lord from all the idols of false gods. In other words, he "cleaned house." He got rid of what amounted to stench in God's nostrils and poison to human souls. By doing so, he invoked God's blessings on himself.

I formerly loved thriller movies and TV shows, even those that bordered on horror. But I knew it was deterring my relationship with Jesus. So I stopped watching such shows and movies and filled the absence with spending quality time in daily devotion. I can tell you that I have a better mind, one that is more in tune with Christ.

> "I will not set before my eyes anything that is worthless." (Psalm 101:3a)
> "Therefore, preparing your minds for action, and being sober-minded, set your hope

fully on the grace that will be brought to you at the revelation of Jesus Christ." (1 Peter 1:13)

"We destroy arguments and every lofty opinion raised against the knowledge of God, and take every thought captive to obey Christ." (2 Corinthians 10:5)

"For those who live according to the flesh set their minds on the things of the flesh, but those who live according to the Spirit set their minds on the things of the Spirit. For to set the mind on the flesh is death, but to set the mind on the Spirit is life and peace." (Romans 8:5–6)

"And you shall love the Lord your God with all your heart and with all your soul and with all our *mind* and with all your strength." (Mark 12:30 (emphasis added)

"Do not be conformed to this world, but be transformed by the renewal of your mind, that by testing you may discern what is the will of God, what is good and acceptable and perfect." (Romans 12:2)

"Set your minds on things that are above, not on things that are on earth." (Colossians 3:2)

"Be sober-minded; be watchful. Your adversary the devil prowls around like a roaring lion, seeking someone to devour." (1 Peter 5:8)

The last verse speaks of a "sober" mind. I believe this is much more than just not getting drunk. You can remain sober mentally yet not remain sober spiritually. To be sober spiritually means to have a clear, clean mind that is not clamored by the garbage and poison of this world. Such a mind can quickly discern the instruction and wisdom readily provided by the Holy Spirit.

If you have trouble with intrusive, ungodly thoughts, take inventory of what you allow in your mind. Discontinue any poison, limit the junk, spend quality time daily in prayer and Bible reading, and read these verses out loud and proclaim the positive of those verses for yourself, several times a day if necessary. Having the mind of Christ will enable you to make wise decisions and hear the voice of the Holy Spirit.

Questions for Reflection:

1. Is there any spiritual "poison" in your life that needs to be eliminated?
2. Is there any spiritual "junk food" in your life that needs to be limited?
3. What does being spiritually "sober minded" mean to you?

Chapter V
Hearing God's Voice

"For he is our God, and we are the people of his pasture, and the sheep of his hand. Today, if you hear his voice, do not harden your hearts." (Psalm 95:7–8a)

"When he has brought out all his own, he goes before them, and the sheep follow him, for they know his voice. A stranger they will not follow, but they will flee from him, for they do not know the voice of strangers." (John 10:4–5)

God knows what is best. He sees the future and knows what lies ahead. He wants to warn us of danger. He wants to give clear direction and guidance. His voice is all around. He speaks, but we often do not recognize His voice.

"The voice of the Lord is over the waters; the God of glory thunders, the Lord, over many waters. The voice of the Lord is powerful; the voice of the Lord is full of majesty. The voice of the Lord breaks the cedars; the Lord breaks the cedars of Lebanon." (Psalm 29:3–5)

"To him who rides in the heavens, the ancient heavens; behold, he sends out his voice, his mighty voice." (Psalm 68:33)

One of my favorite things to watch is aerial skiing where skiers zoom down a steep ramp which suddenly turns upward, catapulting the skier way up in the air. On the descent down, the skier performs acrobatic twists and flips. During one competition, I heard the announcer say, "There's the coach's voice." The announcer kept saying this during several jumps. I turned up the TV. But all I could hear was cheering and cow bells. Not one voice was distinguishable over the others, not as far as I was concerned. But the skiers are able to distinguish their coach's voice. They know his voice from spending many hours a day with him (or her). Certain jumps require bent knees. But once they are in the air, the skier does not know which is up or down. The skier relies on the coach to tell him/her when to straighten the knees. Skiers are disciplined athletes who can tune out the distraction and focus on the voice of their coach.

How many times do we miss God's voice because of the other voices/thoughts loudly and rudely dominating our brain? This world offers many distractions. Having the mind of Christ as described in the previous chapter will better equip you to distinguish Jesus's voice from all the other voices.

I'm a big fan of car racing. It may seem like an individual sport, but it's not. All team members are crucial. The driver depends on the pit crew to change tires and refuel the car quickly while the crew chief calculates fuel mileage and decides when to bring the car in for refueling. The driver depends heavily on the spotter who tells the driver if he is clear to make a pass or if another driver is coming around him. Wrecks happen frequently which may occur around a turn where a driver is unable to see. But the spotter is usually able to see a wreck before the driver and informs him to go high or low on the track in order to avoid the wreck. Sometimes, there may not be time to explain, "There's been a wreck on turn four; you need to go high on the track." The spotter may simply say, "Go high! Go high!" The driver needs to be prepared to respond immediately to avoid the wreck.

God is our spotter. He knows what lies ahead; that's why it is so critical to listen to Him even if we do not know His reason. Of course, wrecks do not take God by surprise. He has known from the beginning of eternity what will happen tomorrow. He does not reveal everything about the future. He tells us what we need to know. He gives us sufficient information. It is up to us to respond to His direction. We need to trust Him. A lot of times, we may not even know the wreck from which we were spared.

Several years ago, I was working a job that God had provided and I enjoyed. But after less than a year on the job, I left for other employment that paid a lot more money. I did not consult God for His will in the situation. I just wanted the money. But that turned out to be a disaster. I worked around the clock. Things did not go well. I went to a few other jobs in the same line of work but none were better. The only jobs that hired me were the same type work. I had the same experience at every place. I was burned out and exhausted with life itself. I was miserable. I had a clean working record and good references from supervisors but was unable to get into a good working situation. That was a prodigal time in my life. I remained stubborn and distant from God, disobedient and sinful, not going to Him in prayer or Bible reading. God let me wander in the wilderness for that time to learn and grow. Years later when I came to my senses, I returned to God, repented and renewed a daily walk with him. After eleven years, I finally found employment in the same field that I never should have left. I could have saved myself a lot of pain and trouble if I had sought God's will and listened to Him all along.

For a few years, I commuted to work with a coworker who had two young children. We loved snow days. We were able to wear jeans to work. We were allowed to arrive a few hours late. We would stop and get coffee on the way. One winter day when the roads were slushy from melting snow we came across a woman who had wrecked her car. We picked her up and carried her to town. My friend was driving. Before the stranded motorist got into the car, something inside me told me to get into the back with the children. But I dismissed the thought and rode in the front. We had a long slow drive ahead of us in the snow before we could reach civilization. After a few miles, the woman started cursing profusely. The only thing that stopped her from cursing was an asthma attack. The incident left two young children shocked and uncomfortable. Of course, I had no idea that the long ride would unfold in such a way. But Jesus knew. It was His voice that I heard telling me to get into the back seat and allow the stranger to ride in the front. I failed those children by not listening to His voice when I could have made them more comfortable by putting space between them and an angry stranger. Even though I would not have brought as much comfort as sitting next to their mother, sitting next to me, an adult they knew and trusted, would have eased the tension they felt on that long ride while they learned all kinds of new colorful words.

Part of learning to hear the voice of God is learning from mistakes. Recognizing where you have missed the voice of God, such as I did in the previous situations, will help you to better recognize His voice in the future.

Not long ago, a woman I knew was going to speak to a man about a certain situation. I did not know much about the man or if he had any propensity to violence. But something inside me told me the man would become very violent. So I called the police and expressed my concern. They immediately responded just as the man started to get violent and took him away in handcuffs before he was able to hurt anyone.

If you are not sure if something you hear is from God or not, ask yourself: "Is this thought/idea in line with God's word?" If it goes against God's word, you can disregard it. God will not go against His word written in the Bible. If it does not go against His word, ask yourself: "Does this sound like something that could possibly be from the Lord, or does this sound like something the devil would want?" When I heard something inside me telling me to give up thriller stories and stories about gruesome murder, I knew it must be from God because the devil would not encourage me to forfeit such shows. It sounded more like God than the devil. Perhaps most importantly, ask God if the thought is from Him or not. Your heavenly Father desires to speak to you and give you direction.

For myself, I have learned that fear and vain thoughts about all the bad possibilities that can happen is not from God. However, when faced with an important decision, like a job for instance, if I feel not fear but an uneasiness deep inside about taking a job, that is

God speaking to me warning me not to take the job. I have learned to listen to that voice. I have heard a number of people in horrible marriage situations say that before they were married, they "knew" that they should not have married that person. I believe that was God speaking.

One of my best friends was murdered at a young age. The guilty are currently serving a life sentence. She was a Christian and positively influenced my relationship with Christ. At first, I wondered why God allowed her to die so young and violently. He could have stopped it.

I had been friends with her since elementary school. After high school, I moved away, and we lost touch for a few years but reignited our friendship the last year of her life. The main thing I remember about her through high school was the fact that she always said that Jesus was coming back soon. She was very smart and did well in school. She earned a living and depended on no one. But she never pursued a college education because she did not believe there was time due to Jesus's return. Now it's true that Jesus can return at any time. But with all my heart, I believe that God impressed upon her heart that she would not have much time on this earth as an adult. Because she believe that, she kept her heart right with Jesus and lived according to His word. God spoke to her loud and clear from an early age about having a short time on this earth so that she was ready for her homecoming in Heaven when the time came. He saved her soul which is much more important than her life.

A few years after the experience of losing a friend, I worked as an investigative social worker for child protective services. My relationship with the Lord was far from where it should have been. But I was trying to develop a better relationship with Him while struggling with letting go of the sin and junk in my life. For the sake of the children God would speak to me even though I didn't realize at the time that it was Him. There were many times while I was interviewing that I just knew something was wrong; but nothing was obvious. People say the most random things when being interviewed. They would say things that appeared to be innocent. A thought would come into my head, "Don't let that go. Ask them..." So I would ask all the questions that popped into my head, applying subtle pressure until the truth (usually) surfaced. I became very skilled at asking follow-up questions. In addition, to just "knowing" that something was wrong, God (although I did not realize it was Him at the time) opened up my eyes to observe body language. I saw nuances between their body language and words. I read books on body language and discovered that the nuances I observed were indeed indicative of lying. So I would dig further in those cases. As a result, I was a thorough investigator. I believe that my case decisions were accurate. It's all because I listened to God.

I remember one particular case. Though not audibly, something inside me screamed, and I mean screamed, to me loud and clear that the dad was guilty. I thought well of the man. He appeared to be an outstanding citizen and great dad. He had a great job. I had nothing against him and did not want him to be guilty. But I just knew that he had committed a serious crime against one of the children. But there was absolutely nothing that tied him to anything wrong. I thought, *No way!* I asked all the right questions and interviewed all the right people but still received no viable information. I closed my case. A few months later, another case came in regarding the same family. Only this time there was stone-cold solid evidence against the dad. I did my job right the first time; I just didn't have all the information. When this new evidence came to light, I realized that voice I had dismissed and said, "No way!" was God. I often wondered why God allowed me to hear His voice that day saying that the dad was guilty when there was nothing I could do about it at the time. With the new evidence, the case was substantiated regardless of whether I heard God's voice or not. But I believe He spoke to me at that time in order to acclimate me to hearing His voice and learn to recognize when He is speaking.

As part of every case, I was required to ask about guns in the home, just to make sure they were locked away and not accessible to children. In one particular home when I asked that question, the man took out his gun (not required and not asked of him) and pointed the barrel at me, waving it back and forth about one foot away from my face. Without thinking, I immediately said, "Thank you for showing me the gun. You can put it away now." He put the gun away. I never felt fear. At the time I could not understand why I remained so calm. I certainly did not know from where those words came. As I said, I never thought about the words before I spoke; they just came out of my mouth as if someone else were speaking. I surprised myself with the response. Looking back, I realize that it could only be from the Lord. Even though my relationship with Him was not where it should have been, His hand was on my life, and I heard His voice. Fortunately in those instances, I listened even though I did not realize it was God speaking.

Hearing God is not only for my benefit. Sometimes, God speaks to me in order to bless others. There are many times when I know that something is wrong with someone in my life. I don't know because anyone has told me anything. It's not a "feeling," it's just a "knowing" deep inside. So I will inquire with the person of whom I am concerned. When the individual opens up, God brings to my mind words of encouragement and scriptures to share. Then I pray for him or her. I don't always pray with the person, but I will pray later.

I remember late one night, someone I knew came to mind. I was not praying at the time, but I knew that I needed to pray for him. Without talking to him, I just prayed. The next day, I learned that he had been attacked and left for dead the previous evening. He was found unconscious but breathing. He received the necessary medical treatment and recovered. That was God speaking when I knew that he needed prayer.

Sometimes when I am praying, someone that I barely know or have not thought about in years will come to my mind. So I pray for those people even though I do not know their circumstance. Sometimes I never hear from them and never know their need. But I believe that God instructs me to pray for them; I don't think that they randomly popped into my head while I was praying. Even though I may never know their need or the outcome of my prayer, God knows.

At my current job, we use two-way transceiver radios. As long as I have my radio on the right channel, I can hear the communication that comes across that channel and others can hear me. If I switch it to a different channel, I cannot transmit or receive any communication. Spiritually, we stay on the same channel as Jesus when we have the mind of Christ, stay in close fellowship with Him and are careful about what we allow in our minds. Isaiah 30: 21 says, "And your ears shall hear a word behind you, saying, 'This is the way, walk in it' when you turn to the right or when you turn to the left."

I know that in my own life, even since I have been making a purposeful intent to walk closely with God, there have been times when I have missed or dismissed God's voice which caused me to stumble. But I quickly get back on track by praying and refocus on Jesus. I am better prepared to hear the next instruction from God.

Distractions are all around trying to take our focus off Jesus and drown out His voice. Even well-meaning friends can lead us in the wrong direction. We often like to talk to people about our problems, some of us more than others. When we do, people love to give advice. There have been a few times in my life when I have been given the wrong advice from friends who intended to help. I have known of several people who have been given the wrong advice from others. Friends do not always know what is best. They certainly do not know the future. They may not be thinking from God's perspective. I'm not saying there is anything wrong with confiding in others and even listening to their advice. But be very careful to whom you listen. I have even been given advice from "friends" who did not mean well and tried to persuade me to take a certain direction in life even when I did not seek or want their advice. The first and main person we need to be consulting is God Almighty. We need His direction and guidance above all else. We need to listen to His voice. He holds the answer and solution to every problem. "Put not your trust in princes, in a son of man, in whom there is no salvation" (Psalm 146:3). "It is better to take refuge in the Lord than to trust in man" (Psalm 118:8). Having a clear mind focused on Jesus will help us hear His voice and tune out others.

"The voice of the Lord flashes forth flames of fire. The voice of the Lord shakes the wilderness" (Psalm 29:7–8a). The voice of the Lord is powerful and mighty. Psalm 29 makes it clear that He speaks.

The question is whether or not we are listening. Listening is not a passive activity. It requires focus and effort. Sometimes after prayer and Bible reading, we just need to be still in quietness and give God the opportunity to speak.

Questions for Reflection

1. Name a time when you heard God's voice speaking to you.
   A. Did you obey? If so, what was the result?
   B. If you disobeyed, what was the result?

2. What distractions hinder you from better hearing God's voice?

Chapter VI
When You've Done Everything Right and the Storm Still Comes

"When you pass through the waters, I will be with you; and through the rivers, they shall not overwhelm you; when you walk through the fire you shall not be burned, and the flame shall not consume you." (Isaiah 43:2)

We can reduce some storms and be better prepared for storms. But the truth is that we are not going to get out of this life without them. Not every storm is the result of discipline or veering off God's path for your life. The Bible does not promise the Christian an easy life. It does not say that God will spare us from all tragedies, hardship, or struggles. Read again the above referenced passage from Isaiah. Notice that it does not say that we will be spared from problems. On the contrary, it sounds as if we can expect them.

On one occasion while working as a social worker, I was standing on the front porch of a client's home talking to someone in the living room. All of a sudden, I felt a sharp pain on my left thigh. As I turned to look, I saw a full-grown pit bull walking by. Before he bit me, I didn't even know a dog was anywhere around. He had bitten me without any warning in order to tell me that if he saw me as a threat, he would attack me.

This scared me much more than the gun, partly because there was pain this time. But even before this happened, given the choice,

I would rather be shot than mauled by a dog. He was a big pit bull, and I knew it would be over if he knocked me down.

Although I was talking to the owner of the dog, he shut the door when the dog bit me, leaving me alone with my attacker. I called out to the owner for help with his dog. But he only opened the door and pretended to call the dog inside, then shut the door and went back inside. Alone on the porch with the dog, I was afraid to move since it might trigger the dog to see me as prey. I called out to the owner a second time, but he never opened the door and only responded by saying the dog outside with me was not the dog who bit me (which was a lie). This was a very rural area, and no one else was around. No cars were driving by. My panic and fear was rapidly rising. I knew the man inside would not help me. I was afraid if I kept calling out the dog might see me as a threat and attack. I knew that I could not hide the anxiety and fear in my voice. I didn't want to move and give the dog a reason to chase. But I also knew that I could not stay on the porch. I said a quick prayer and slowly walked to my car. The dog did not attack. I made it to the car and called 911 (I should have had my phone with me in the first place rather than leaving it in the car).

The Sheriff's Deputy who responded must have been having a bad day. He fussed at me for getting bit, saying that I should have known better because I was the third person that dog had bitten. I told him, "Excuse me, but I'm injured and that is bad enough. Don't talk to me like that anymore." He profusely apologized. That incident was not from God's discipline or reaping what I sowed. It was just part of living in this world.

Why? Why? Why? Why does God allow tragedy and problems when I'm living right? There are many reasons. We may not even know the reason while residing on this earth. We live in a fallen world. 1 Peter 5:8 describes the devil as a "roaring lion, seeking someone to devour." As much as God loves you, the devil hates you. He will get at you any way he can. Believe me, he works nonstop vehemently against God's children. In Matthew 24:9, Jesus warned His followers that they will be hated among the nations which is the whole world. 2 Corinthians 2:15–16 describes Christians as the "aroma of life" to other people who are saved and to those who are not saved, we are the "fragrance of death." The friction this causes is not conducive to living an easy life. Regardless of why problems occur or from where they come, life on this earth involves losses and tragedy. Things just happen that are beyond our control. Situations arise that the individual does not deserve. We give too much credit to why. Knowing why does not make things easier or make the problem go away quicker.

There are storms that God does not cause but allows us to experience. Although it may not feel like it at the time, we will be better off as a result. Storms refine our relationship with God. They sift through the muck on the inside and bring to the surface things that need to be dealt with. They cause us to spend more time on our knees, thus enriching our relationship with the Lord. The incident with the dog caused me to evaluate my relationship with the Lord and made me question whether I was ready for my life to end and meet Jesus face to face. When I was alone with the dog on the porch, I really thought that my life was going to end that day.

As James 1:2–4 says, "Count it all joy, my brothers, when you meet trials of various kinds, for you know that the testing of your faith produces steadfastness. And let steadfastness have its full effect, that you may be perfect and complete, lacking in nothing."

The early church was no stranger to trials and suffering. The same message from the previously mentioned verse in James is found throughout the New Testament to encourage not only the early believers but us today:

> "Not only that, but we rejoice in our sufferings, knowing that suffering produces endurance, and endurance produces character, and character produces hope, and hope does not put us to shame, because God's love has been poured into our hearts through the Holy Spirit who has been given to us." (Romans 5:3–5)
>
> "For I consider that the sufferings of this present time are not worth comparing with the glory that is to be revealed to us." (Romans 8:18)

"Beloved, do not be surprised at the fiery trial when it comes upon you to test you, as though something strange were happening to you. But rejoice insofar as you share Christ's sufferings, that you may also rejoice and be glad when his glory is revealed." (1 Peter 4:12–13)

Suffering is not something to fear. The early church did not undergo light sufferings. They experienced great persecution. In 2 Corinthians 11:25, the Apostle Paul described being beaten, stoned and shipwrecked. He wrote many letters giving encouragement and instruction to early Christians while he was imprisoned. So the verses that describe sufferings are not talking about mere nuisances but real sufferings. As you read through the following verses, notice that each one seems to describe suffering as something to look forward to and even rejoice over.

"That I may know him and the power of his resurrection, and may share his sufferings, becoming like him in his death." (Philippians 3:10)

"Now I rejoice in my sufferings for your sake, and in my flesh I am filling up what is lacking in Christ's afflictions for the sake of his body, that is, the church." (Colossians 1:24)

"Therefore do not be ashamed of the testimony about our Lord, nor of me his prisoner, but share in suffering for the gospel by the power of God." (2 Timothy 1:8)

The reason we can "rejoice" over suffering is the good that it produces. The fruit that comes from suffering may not be so evident in this lifetime. But it prepares unimaginable blessings awaiting us in Heaven by keeping us in the best possible relationship with Jesus, the Savior.

Through these verses, God is encouraging believers to accept sufferings as a way of life and not be discouraged by it. Just keep going. Keep moving forward. Don't allow it to stop you. "We are afflicted in every way, but not crushed; perplexed, but not driven to despair; persecuted, but not forsaken; struck down, but not destroyed" (2 Corinthians 4:8–9).

The real question is not why but what. What is my response going to be to this situation? Will it be one of trust? Will it be one of praise despite difficult times? Will it be one of seeking God's guidance? Or will my response be to turn away from God? Will I chose bitterness instead of praise and trust? Storms tend to either push people toward God or away from God. If we will turn toward God and trust Him, we will grow from the experience and become closer to Him, who has our life on this earth and our eternal life in His hands.

Questions for Reflection

1. What is your personal attitude toward hard/difficult times?
2. Do you tend to turn toward God or away from God during difficult times?
3. What is the result from turning toward (or away) from God?

Chapter VII
The Good Soldier and Athlete

"Share in suffering as a good soldier of Christ Jesus." (2 Timothy 2:3)

The Bible compares the Christian life to that of a soldier (2 Timothy 2:3 and 4) which does not paint the picture of an easy life. Soldiers endure tough, rigorous, exhaustive hard core training in order to be ready for battle. In basic training, they run and exercise frequently. They suffer serious consequences if they do not listen to their commanding officer. They also learn different assignments and how to work together. The training is a discipline (remember the definition of discipline from chapter II) that invokes a new way of thinking which leads to doing things that go against one's natural way of thinking. But the new discipline makes the soldiers ready for battle. Soldiers would not do well in battle if they were slow, sluggish and out of shape. Neither would they do well in battle if they had no discipline or leadership.

My dad was in the 82nd Airborne Division in the Army. He told me once that learning to jump out of helicopters began by being told to jump off a chair and not land on his feet. No one wants to fall and get bruised. But if your commanding officer tells you to jump and not land on your feet, you better do it. What may seem unreasonable can often have good reason. When we see shows of people parachuting, they land on their feet. But landing on the feet risks a broken leg. A broken leg puts yourself and your comrades in jeopardy when you are in enemy territory.

I cannot imagine jumping out of a plane; the thought terrifies me. So I asked my dad once how he overcame the fear of jumping out of a plane. He replied, "You don't. The guy behind you pushes you out."

As soldiers for Christ, we are warned in 2 Timothy 2:4 (NIV), "No one serving as a soldier gets entangled in civilian affairs, but rather tries to please his commanding officer." This coincides with living a life of obedience and being careful what we allow in our minds as discussed in chapter IV. The more we are devoted to the life of a good soldier of Christ, the more pleasing we are to Jesus, our Commanding Officer.

A soldier has a disciplined mind. He does not shy away from battle but faces it bravely with the training he has received. He is not caught by surprise by being placed in the battle; he knew the day may come when he signed up. He follows the orders of his commanding officer. Is that not like the Christian life? When we accepted Jesus as Savior, we signed up to be in His army. It is an army because the devil is constantly waging war. But we have a victorious Commanding Officer in Jesus. I would rather stand with Jesus and be in the midst of the battle than spare myself from any of the devil's arrows by standing with the enemy. The ultimate victory is with Jesus.

As our Commanding Officer, Jesus equips us for battle. He provides us with all the armor we need as described in Ephesians 6:10–18: the belt of truth, the breastplate of righteousness; shoes that keep us steady to live out the gospel of peace; the shield of faith; the helmet of salvation; and the Sword of the Spirit which is the word of God. Having the right armor will enable us to withstand the storms of life as the battle rages.

Let's take a closer look at each piece of armor. A belt wraps around the core of the body. To me, the belt of truth signifies being wrapped by truth and being centered by truth—the truth of the Gospel of Christ. A breastplate protects against an attack. As discussed previously, obedient (righteous) living brings us under God's protection and blessing and endears Him to be attentive to our prayers (2 Chronicles 16:9). Proper shoes not only protect the feet but provide support to the back and legs, making a long journey more bearable. I stand firm on the gospel of peace which is Jesus Christ as I journey through this life. My faith in God is my shield that I hold up to protect me from all the attacks of the enemy. I have seen God's faithfulness. I believe His word. I trust Him. A helmet protects the head. With my helmet of salvation, I protect my mind and thinking by what I allow in my mind. Notice that all the armor so far is for defense. This is what we have for protection. We are given one offensive weapon: the Sword of the Spirit which is the Word of God. Speak Scripture, God's word, out loud. Proclaim God's promises over a situation. Give God praise and glory. Tell Him who He is: the awesome Creator and King of the universe for starters. Then go from there, whatever your heart tells you to proclaim. God's word brings new life to a depressing situation and light where once there was only darkness. Utilize the Sword of the Spirit in the midst of the storm. The more you speak God's word out loud, the more the enemy loses his power over you. The Word, or Sword, is the only offensive weapon we need. The battle is the Lord's. He will move and act on our behalf. Our enemy the devil was struck with a fatal blow the day Jesus rose from the dead. In his limited days, the devil tries to grab hold and torment any way he can. Cut his grip with the Sword of the Spirit.

For many years, I suffered from severe depression and unrelenting fear. There were times that fear was so intense that I thought it had me by the throat choking me and wouldn't let go. I felt as if fear grabbed my heart and squeezed it making it beat faster. I felt as if everything was hopeless. I literally felt as if I were doomed to hell and could not be saved. I thought that God would never help me. I would sob uncontrollably for hours. I was prescribed a lot of medication and was even told by a psychiatrist that I would need the medication for the rest of my life. The medication helped to alleviate the symptoms but did not take away the hopelessness. A day that I didn't feel hopeless in this life and doomed for eternity was a good day for me. It was like seeing a dim light at the end of a very dark tunnel. I cried out to God for help. I knew that I could never have any quality of life in such a state. In His mercy, He led me to someone who led me in prayers of forgiving others as well as myself and prayers of release from the depression and fear. That was the beginning of seeing the enemy defeated in my life. I no longer suffered from intense depression or fear. Not long after, I got off the medication. For anyone reading this who is on medication, please consult with your medical provider before stopping medication. I am not advocating going against medical recommendations. I am not saying there is anything wrong with medication. For myself, I just did not want to be on the medication. I replaced the medication with a lot prayer, praise, and Bible reading. For several months after, depression and fear would try to worm their way back into my life. I fought against it with the Sword of the Spirit, the Word of God. I claimed that it would not come on me in the name of Jesus. I praised God. I quoted Scriptures. Each time I did that, the depression and fear loosened its grip. Each time it came back, it had less of a grip. I would use the Sword again until eventually it left me alone. I very rarely feel the hand of depression or fear. They pretty much leave me alone. I never put away my Sword. Whether things are going good or bad, I use my Sword every day. None of the armor should be taken off. We never know what attack may come or from where. It's best to always stay prepared even when we feel that things are going well.

The Bible also compares the Christian life to an athlete (1 Corinthians 9:25 and 2 Timothy 2:5), who like soldiers, are subjected to many hours of intense training. I love watching the Olympics. I enjoy the background stories of the competitors. They get up early to work out and practice. They spend many hours in exhaustive training. They stay up late. Many of them are still in school and have to incorporate their school work into their day. They are not able to eat anything they want; they have to be very careful of their diet. They often miss out on fun activities. They devote almost their whole day to their sport. They give up an easy life for the chance of a medal. Some even know that they are not in the same league as the top athletes, but they still remain focused and devote their lives to the sport. Just to be at the Olympics is such a great honor to them.

Both athletes and soldiers receive medals. The best medal of all is the crown of life God gives to those who have stood the trials of life and endured. "Blessed is the man who remains steadfast under trial, for when he has stood the test he will receive the crown of life, for which God has promised to those who love him" (James 1:12).

Hardships and adversity separate true believers, people who are truly committed to their relationship to Jesus, from people who are not committed to Jesus, who have not submitted to His Lordship. If I shrink back from my belief and commitment to Jesus as a result of a painful trial, I need to examine the motives of my heart and ask myself, "What does Jesus mean to me?" "Is He just 'fire insurance' because I don't want to go to hell?" "Is He just a 'genie in a bottle' to me who is here to grant my requests?" On the other hand, if I retain my faith under pressure and understand that Jesus is Lord and should be praised no matter what happens, my motive for receiving Jesus as Savior is laid bare for all to see.

Having said that, please let me make it clear that sincere Christians will still experience pain, hurt, and even anger as a result of hard times. We are not immune from the emotions of this world. But if we pray and allow God to bring us through hard times, we will be shaped by His handiwork, not the emotions.

If we view life as being here to benefit God's Kingdom, to be His servant rather than needing life to please us at every possible moment, we will not get as discouraged and sidetracked from disappointments and troubles. Whether storms are minor or tragic, I believe God will help us heal quicker and recover faster when we turn to Him and trust Him. That is easier to do when we have our mind on Him in the first place because we have been through the discipline of a soldier or athlete for Christ and are equipped for battle with the proper armor.

Questions for Reflection

1. How does discipline now help to prepare us for future problems?
2. Name a time in your life when you have benefited from the result of discipline.
3. What does the "crown of life" mentioned in James 1:12 mean to you?
4. According to James 1:12, how do we receive the crown of life?

Chapter VIII
Comfort

"Keep listening to my words, and let this be your comfort." (Job 21:2)

When we turn to God, He comforts us. He brings peace. One of the biggest advantages we have as children of God is having access to the sweet peace and comfort He has to offer. Psalm 30:5 says, "For his anger is but for a moment, and his favor is for a lifetime. Weeping may tarry for the night, but joy comes with the morning."

Perhaps the old hymn, What a Friend We Have in Jesus (words written by Joseph M. Scriven) says it best:

"What a Friend we have in Jesus,
All our sins and griefs to bear!
What a privilege to carry
Everything to God in prayer!
O what peace we often forfeit,
O what needless pain we bear,
All because we do not carry
Everything to God in prayer!"[2]

Truly, how much comfort and peace do we miss because we do not commit everything to God in prayer? Turning to God in times of suffering, tragedy, and loss will bring healing quicker. It does not mean that we will never experience the sting again. But when we turn to God, the sting of pain has to go through Jesus first before it reaches us. Jesus is our guard, our armor. He is our comfort.

> "You will increase my greatness and comfort me again." (Psalm 71:21)
>
> "This is my comfort in my affliction, that your promise gives me life." (Psalm 119:50)
>
> "Let your steadfast love comfort me according to your promise to your servant." (Psalm 119:76)
>
> "You will say in that day: 'I will give thanks to you, O Lord, for though you were angry with me, your anger turned away, that you might comfort me'." (Isaiah 12:1)
>
> "Sing for joy, O heavens, and exult O earth; break forth, O mountains, into singing! For the Lord has comforted his people and will have compassion on his afflicted." (Isaiah 49:13)

If you are going through times of heartache and pain, recite the preceding verses out loud. Ask God for his comfort and peace.

I do not believe that God brings afflictions on His people for the benefit of someone else. I certainly do not believe that God allows tragedy or the loss of a loved one as discipline or for the good of other people. But God gives his comfort to help you. And in turn, you have the opportunity to be a blessing to others by sharing the comfort you have received from the Lord to help others in similar situations. You can be an extension of God's healing hand. All of us are more able to be helped by someone who has gone through a similar experience as opposed to someone who has no idea what we are going through. "Who comforts us in all our affliction, so that we may be able to comfort those who are in any affliction, with the comfort with which we ourselves are comforted by God. For as we share abundantly in Christ's sufferings, so through Christ we share abundantly in comfort too" (2 Corinthians 1:4–5). I believe that reaching out and being a blessing to others brings healing faster.

Questions for Reflection

1. Have you ever experienced comfort?
2. Have you ever talked to someone who had experienced a similar troubling situation as you? If so, were you helped?
3. Has someone ever talked to you about a similar situation that you have experienced?

Chapter IX
The Deep

"He gathers the waters of the sea into jars; he puts the deep into storehouses." (Psalm 33:7, NIV)

I probably read through the Psalms many times before I ever noticed the above verse. But as I read it one day, I saw a picture of several mason jars filled with water in God's store house in heaven. Then like a movie that backtracks to show you how they got there, I saw a hand scooping the jars, one by one, down into the ocean's depths until all the seas and all the oceans were emptied. The water in that verse represents pressure.

Swimming in a few feet of water is no problem and feels good. I can swim straight down in nine feet of water. But after much more than nine feet my ears start hurting if I swim straight down. In order to swim down to twelve feet, I have to descend at an angle rather than straight. It's because of the pressure of the water. Water has weight. The further down you go, the more the weight increases.

Once you transcend the surface of the sea and go down to the depths of the ocean, the pressure is really on. I wanted to know how far a human could withstand the intense pressure before being crushed, so I punched the question into the internet search engine which took me to www.medicaldaily.com/breaking-point-how-much-water-pressure-can-human-body-take-347570.

As the site explained, scientists can't give a set answer to that question since it would require experiments of sending people to their deaths. OK, fair enough. After all, I certainly would not volunteer for that experiment. But it also said that most professional free divers do not go lower than 400 feet deep. As the site further explained, the weight of the water above the diver increases by 15 pounds every 33 feet the diver descends. Pressure underneath water is greater than pressure in the human body. Underneath 100 feet of water the spongy lung tissue contracts, not allowing as much oxygen. A "dive response" then takes over, restricting blood to the limbs in order for more blood to flow to the heart and lungs. The blood vessels in the chest expand to counterbalance the pressure from the water.[3]

The deepest place on earth is the Mariana Trench in the Pacific Ocean. To understand it more, I went to Wikipedia on the internet. The following information comes from http://en.wikipedia.org/wiki/Mariana_Trench: The Mariana (or Marianas) Trench is roughly 1580 miles long and 43 miles wide with a depth of 36,070 feet. The southern end has a valley called the Challenger Deep which reaches a depth of 36,201 feet. To put that in perspective, if you were to move Mt. Everest and place it in the Mariana Trench, Mt. Everest would still be covered by a mile of water. Also according to the Wikipedia site, at the bottom of the trench, the human body would feel 1000 times more standard atmospheric pressure than at sea level. We would be crushed, literally.[4]

The problems and storms of this life drag us down, as if anchoring us to a weight that slowly pulls us toward the abyss of despair and hopelessness. We feel the crushing weight of insurmountable problems that squeeze from every side and want to break our bones, crush our skull, and collapse our lungs. But cry out to God, listen to His voice. Trust Him. We will find that we are not crushed; we are not overtaken. We are saved. God has released the pressure by gathering up the sea of problems and releasing us from its weight as he brings our problems to His storehouse. Each jar of water, or problems, that He gathers bring us up closer to the surface, closer to Him. The closer we are to Him, the higher above the waves we rise.

> "But they who wait for the Lord shall renew their strength; they shall mount up with wings like eagles" (Isaiah 40:31a).

Questions for Reflection

1. What problems are you currently facing that weigh you down?
2. Write the problems on a sheet of paper and pray about each one. Thank God ahead of time for His solution.

Chapter X
Our Belay System

"He made my feet like the feet of a deer and set me secure on the heights." (Psalm 18:33)

Many years ago, I completed a high elements ropes course thirty feet in the air. Now keep in mind that I am very afraid of heights. Before I began the endeavor, I had to strap into a harness that was part of a belay system, the system that would catch me if I fell, the system that was literally the difference between life and death or at the very least severe injury. A person on the ground held on to a rope that was hooked on to my harness as I climbed the ladder to a platform that awaited me thirty very long feet up in the air. As I made the ascent, I kept saying over and over in my mind, "My belay system's got me. My belay system's got me." But saying that and knowing that did nothing to comfort me. I could not feel the support of the belay system, so I was not comforted by the knowledge that it was there. I made it to the platform. As instructed, I hooked into another belay system above the platform which was a rope suspended from a cable that ran along the tree tops. I even remembered to hook into the second belay system before unhooking the belay system attached to the person on the ground. "Because," as we were warned before starting the course, "If you unhook from one rope before securing yourself to the next rope, a bee might fly by and you might swat at it and fall to the ground." That almost did me in when I heard that. They were combining my two worst fears: heights and bees.

For the first element, I had to walk sideways across a loose rope that swayed so bad that the only way to make it across was to hold on to the rope in front that was a little higher and parallel to the rope on which I walked. But the rope was low and forced me to lean forward looking at the ground. Being on top and looking down, the distance seems much higher than being on the ground and looking to the top of the trees. My right leg was shaking. I was so scared. Again, I kept telling myself, "My belay system's got me. My belay system's got me." But again, that did nothing to comfort me. And again I could not feel the support of the belay system. When I felt as if I could no longer bear to look at the ground, I stood up straight in order to look forward. As soon as I did, the rope I was walking across swung forward. My feet were still touching the rope, but they were level with my butt, as if I were sitting in midair. That was the first time I could feel the support of the belay system. When the rope swung out from under my feet, the belay system did its job and caught me, suspending me from the cable above. Someone on the ground told me to bend my knees which enabled me to get my feet under me and complete the element. After that, I had no fear whatsoever for the rest of the course. I had total confidence in the belay system. It caught me once and I knew it would do it again, as many times as necessary.

If we never had any problems, we would never know the strong arm of God. We would never know His power. We would never feel His strength. He is the belay system on this ropes course that we call life. Whether we "feel" Him or not, He is there ready to catch us when we fall.

Remember Isaiah 43:2 where God promises will be with you in the fire and in the water. You will not be burned up, and you will not drown. It may be uncomfortable for a while. But God will bring you through it. He will never leave you nor forsake you.

The second to last element on the ropes course was a rock climbing wall standing forty-five feet high. Once more, I was hooked onto a belay system with a person on the ground holding the rope connected to my harness. I had no rock climbing experience. Twice, I got myself stuck. With every crevice out of my reach, I had nowhere to go. The person on the ground took on all my weight and pulled on the rope which enabled me to reach another crevice and finally scale the wall. Just like the first element, I was unable to feel the belay system until I needed it and the person holding my rope lifted me up. Is that not like God? When we reach that place where there is just nowhere else to go, He lifts us up so that we can secure our grip and keep moving upward. I believe that God intervenes and blesses much more than we realize.

He is always present and always ready. Is there anything too hard for the Creator and Sustainer of the universe? The God who keeps the planets in orbit and created the stars to shine at night is the same God who is ready and able to help you. The best part is that He doesn't have to "brainstorm" and think of a solution. He is not worried about knowing what to do because He already has the answer.

"Cast your cares on the Lord and he will sustain you; he will never let the righteous be shaken." (Psalm 55:22, NIV)

"The Lord is my strength and my shield; my heart trusts in him, and he helps me." (Psalm 28:7a, NIV)

"You are a hiding place for me; you preserve me from trouble; you surround me with shouts of deliverance." (Psalm 32:7)

The last element on the ropes course was a zip line which is a pulley system that slides along a cable. All I had to do was hold on. It was so much fun. I felt pure exhilaration all the way down from the climbing wall. The elation I felt was due in part to the fact that it was just plain fun. But another reason I felt such exhilaration was knowing what I had just accomplished. I felt that I had just conquered a mountain. I felt untouchable. I could not believe that I had survived. The third reason I felt such pure joy was knowing that it was all behind me. I didn't have to worry about bees anymore. I didn't have to worry about getting myself stuck again on the climbing wall. It was all over. The high from that experience lasted a couple of hours.

For the child of God, that's the way this life ends and the next begins. I believe we'll go into Heaven just as elated and overjoyed as my experience on the zip line. That elation and joy will never end because it is Heaven; the high will never go away. We can relax and enjoy eternity because all the trials and problems are behind us. We have completed the course.

Towards the end of his life, the Apostle Paul knew that he had much to look forward to. He went through many struggles during his Christian walk which he described in 2 Corinthians 11:25: beatings, stoning, and a shipwreck. With the Lord as his belay system he mounted the climbing wall. As he stood at the top with his struggles behind and having heaven to look to, he wrote in 2 Timothy 4:6–8:

> "For I am already being poured out as a drink offering, and the time of my departure has come. I have fought the good fight, I have finished the race, I have kept the faith. Henceforth there is laid up for me the crown of righteousness, which the Lord, the righteous judge, will award to me on that day, and not only to me but also to all who have loved his appearing."

The Bible does not specify how Paul died. I searched for his death on the internet and read about it on the first three sites. All three websites: www.christianity.com/.../apostolic-behead-the-death-of-paul-11629583.htm,[5] https://en.wikipedia.org/wiki/Paul_the_Apostle,[6] and www.gotquestions.org/how-did-Paul-die.html[7] concur that he was most likely beheaded, his final storm. Just imagine the homecoming he must have experienced, the joy and elation as he was on his way to seeing Jesus.

Questions for Reflection

1. Has there been a time in your life when you have experienced God's solution for a problem? If so, how did that affect your faith?
2. Share your testimony of God providing a solution to your problem with someone.

Conclusion

Storms are a part of this life. Some storms we create ourselves. This is actually fortunate because it means that we are not helpless. We are not just prey to whatever happens in this life. If we follow biblical principles and seek God's guidance, we can avoid some storms. We have a good amount of control over our lives. We can certainly control what we sow and reap.

God speaks. Psalm 29 speaks of God's voice loud and clear above all the distractions in this life. There are many distractions wanting to draw our attention away from God's voice. But having the mind of Christ enables us to better tune in to the correct frequency to discern God's voice and hear Him above all other voices.

Still some storms are unavoidable and not the fault of the individual. But even in this, we are not defeated and not just prey to the wickedness of this world. We serve a God who is greater than the storm. Whether we cause the storms ourselves or not, growth and a deeper relationship with Jesus can be the result which will ensure eternal blessings. Whatever the reason for the storm, we can grow and learn from it. We can experience God's faithfulness and comfort and in turn comfort others.

You serve the same Lord who reached down and picked up Peter by the hand during the storm. Our God is not deterred by the storms of life. Just as He saved Peter, He will save you. Jesus did not shy away from the cross but faced it head on. Jesus is not afraid of the storms in your life. He will face them with you. He is willing to reach out and personally take your hand to lift you up above the raging waves.

You do not have to be beaten down and conquered by the storm. The devil may be a roaring lion looking for someone to devour (1 Peter 5:8), but Jesus is the Lion of Judah (Revelation 5:5) who rose from the cross and conquered the lion that is looking to devour you.

Prayer

In order to help you see victory in life's storms, I developed a sample prayer:

Dear Lord, I come to you helpless and weak, defeated by life's storms. I realize now that I have tried to survive on my own, and I can't do it. I release control of my life and give it to You. I realize there have been times when I have not listened to You or Your Word. I ask for Your forgiveness for disobedience and all my sins. I thank You for Your forgiveness and receive it now. I thank You that You never intended for me survive life's storms on my own. I ask You to redeem me from my sins and mistakes. Please give me wisdom. Lead me in Your path. Help me to discern Your voice from others. Please help me to keep my focus on You and Your Word in my mind. I choose to trust You as You bring me through the storms of life. I thank You that You have never failed me or let me down, and You never will. Help me to see the blessings You have provided. I thank you for continuing to be with me all the days of my life. In Jesus's name. Amen.

Reference Page

Chapter II

[1] Vine's Complete Expository Dictionary of Old and New Testament Words. W.E. Vine, Merrill F. Unger, William White Jr. 1985, 1996. Thomas Nelson Inc. page 172 in "An Expository Dictionary of New Testament Words with their Precise Meanings for English Readers" by W.E. Vine, M.A. section.

Chapter VIII

[2] URLhttps://library.timelesstruths.org/music/What_a_Friend_We_Have_in_Jesus/
- **Website Title** Blessed Assurance > Lyrics | Frances J. Crosby
- **Article Title** What a Friend We Have in Jesus

Chapter IX

[3] URLhttp://www.medicaldaily.com/breaking-point-how-much-water-pressure-can-human-body-take-347570
- **Website Title** Medical Daily
- **Article Title** Breaking Point: How Much Water Pressure Can The Human Body Take?
- **Date Published** August 13, 2015

[4] URLhttp://en.wikipedia.org/wiki/Mariana_Trench
- **Website Title** Wikipedia
- **Article Title** Mariana Trench

Chapter X

[5] URLwww.christianity.com/.../apostolic-behead-the-death-of-paul-11629583.htm
- **Article Title** Apostolic Beheading; The Death of Paul

[6] **URL** https://en.wikipedia.org/wiki/Paul_the_Apostle
- **Website Title** Wikipedia
- **Article Title** Paul the Apostle

[7] **URL** http://www.gotquestions.org/how-did-Paul-die.html
- **Website Title** GotQuestions.org
- **Article Title** How did the apostle Paul die?

About the Author

 Melissa Berry calls North Carolina home. She grew up in Greensboro, North Carolina, and currently resides in the eastern part of the state. She studied social work at Oral Roberts University and graduated with a degree in psychology from Shaw University. As a social worker, she worked many years with children and families suffering from a wide range of problems including substance use, neglect, and abuse. She has volunteered with domestic violence programs being a first responder to adults and children who were victims of sexual assault. She has been on a mission trip to South Africa and stayed with the Zulu tribe for a few weeks. She enjoys public speaking and teaching. In her spare time, she enjoys photography and hiking. Her hiking trips have included trails in Alaska, Washington State, Oregon, New Mexico, Texas, South Africa, and all over the mountains of North Carolina.

CPSIA information can be obtained
at www.ICGtesting.com
Printed in the USA
FSHW012336160219
55719FS